1

ISBN: 9798847564335

Any similarities to any one named John Streetsmart is purely coincidental. This story is written as told to Lynn Hankins. All names have been changed.

Day 1 1982

It was November 18th at 3:26 am I was born. I do not remember much except for the fact that no one gave a fuck except my grandma. My pops is locked up doing time for a felony. I had to get open heart surgery due to a heart problem I was born with. At the age of 2, I had this surgery. my mother came in to try to claim me, but she could not do anything because she was drunk so my grandma came in and was the strong woman I needed and took custody of me. Me being young I thought my grandma was my mom. One day my grandma asked my mom to come and babysit me. she never showed up. And that is how I got my hood life. the beginning of my story! After that first day, I realized babysitting me was a project. I did not know I was evil and conniving and manipulative and vindictive. I was 3 years old now. Instead of hanging out with my babysitter, I was hanging out with the babysitter's brothers. Hanging out with her brothers I learned how to steal bikes and cars and carry guns.

I could talk nicely to people to get what I wanted. extortion was the key. From that, I learned the neighborhood like Baldwin and Wyandanch and Westbury and others. And from those neighborhoods, I learned how to manipulate the Bronx, Manhattan, Jersey, Brooklyn, Port Washington, Philadelphia, Connecticut, Central Islip, Kentucky, Florida, Oklahoma, and Hawaii. I am only 3 years old, and I am still learning. everything is fun, so you look at it as a kid doing kid stuff. As you get a little older like 4,5 or 6 you learn that you have to fight. you fight to the point that you have to hurt someone until they start bleeding, and you laugh about it. I did not know how to turn this off. As you do these things you still want to be a kid, play in the park and tunnels, and get a little coochie. You do not know what coochie is, but you hear everyone talking about it. You know you can get into a female's head as you are talking to and learning from older guys. And from this, I learned that a man can manipulate a woman's mind if she lets him and that a female has a leash on a man's ego and thoughts, and personality.

That was how I learned that men have ego trips and as a kid, you are not supposed to know about that. that was when the testosterone came in. As older male influencers are supposed to teach you to do better, they do not teach you shit. they teach you how to fight, how to be aggressive and they make you think why the fuck am I here. As a kid, you are not supposed to think about suicide but at 5 and 6 years old that was all that was on my mind. banging your head against concrete, learning that fire and guns are your best friends! Why should you trust anybody? The only thing they are going to do is manipulate you to get what they want from you; I never thought a day in my life that I would be a drug dealer. holding a package for someone at 1 or 2 o'clock in the morning you supposed to be asleep not hanging on the corner next to a park with a wall. I am 9 or 10 years old now and people think I am 13 or 14. You're young as hell walking up and down the streets trying to make a dollar. as someone told me if you going to do something be the best at it. I saw a female getting her ass whipped so I beat up her pimp. She told me I was too young to be out on these streets and that I should go home as I was better than that. As I am walking home, I am taking the backstreets.

A man reached out, grabbed me, and raped me. After that I started drinking and realized stabbing people is really good for you. When you stab someone, it feels so pleasurable. it is like the pain you have inside of you is released from you and you do not think about it anymore. If someone touches you, you jump. And you carry that for the rest of your life. Then you realize that was not the first time you were touched. Your babysitter took advantage of you too. It sounds cool as your babysitter was a female. So now you have grown to rely on fire, knives, and guns. When you learn that you are supposed to protect women you alter the situation. you think differently. A woman has 2 holes to go in, but I only have one. So how do you think I feel now as I am old as shit? Now at age 11, I am more aggressive and disrespectful to basically everyone. in the streets, I am the nicest person but to my family I am rude. I tried to set the house on fire, but I put the fire out. This is the time I realized fire and I have a connection. When you try to set yourself on fire and you are in a place of not understanding and you do not get burned or even scorched but all of your surroundings get burned down. you look at everything around you and you confide in a female and start telling her things and she turns around and takes advantage.

As a child, you do not see it as someone taking advantage of your kindness maybe I was looking for a mother figure. not knowing that she knew exactly what she was doing. She got pregnant. When you feel that you can tell her everything and you look at her and you see her as a mother figure and not a young lady. She was older than me. One day we are laying in her bed, and she took off my clothes and she gave me a bj (oral sex), you do not think it is unnatural as she is not my mother. You teach a 10-year-old boy how to please and treat a female. how to make a female feel like she is the only one. You learn that in every situation you get into with a female you can either learn or fail. The things she taught me allowed me to get some of the baddest women.

By Age 11

I am back hanging with the homies. Testosterone, anger, and aggression teach you how to be the alpha male as a kid. The only way it can be taken is if someone takes it from you. The only way to keep that from happening is to protect the weak and treat them with respect and treat the bullies like prey! You treat the older ones like they are the same age as you are. This made me grow up before my age. I was 5'11 and I had facial hair, so I was in a bar at age 11 and I said I was 21 when someone asked me my age. I was robbing houses by this time. Josh asked me if I wanted to make some money- when I asked doing what he said B and E- I did not know what that meant. He taught me how to divide $. I shared how to make $ without working to make $. I wanted to show them a better path than what had learned- I taught them what I knew, and they took it and ran with it! It still haunts me to this day. Crime pays and $ talks and bullshit walks!! I am extorting grown ass men- grown men move out of my way as I am walking. This is the mindset of my influencers. Not realizing I am a product of them- not thinking you say go and I fly off the handle. Not scared of jail not scared of getting stabbed or shot I begin to realize running thru neighborhoods with this reputation someone is going to test it. People do not fear what they can control or manipulate- they are scared when you have your own independence and your

own mind.

That is where the ass whippings come in. So, you watch. Someone that is doing karate-you are not trying to learn it but rather you are watching the movement. When the session is over you say the last movement you did, I did not understand it. Then he starts to show me the movement so now he is my mentor. One day I was in the park, and someone took my basketball and pushed me down on the ground. I looked at my mentor and asked if I should react. He said no. So, I asked for my ball back. He said yeah you can have it back and throws the ball in my face. A split second later I felt a punch in my face. I looked at my mentor and asked him again and he said yes. So now I choked him out until he cannot breathe, then my mentor had to come to take me off of him. My mentor said he would not teach me anymore, because I have too much aggression and anger. My older cousin had a problem- he pointed and said someone was talking about my mother- he tapped the guy on side of his ribs and hit him once and he fell to the ground unconscious. That was when I realized to hit bricks as hitting people caused bodily harm. No fighting so I became humble as hell! You can say what you want as long as you do not touch me!

Age 12

This is the time females became a big problem. I used my charm, and I would go to outside areas to find females. When they started getting pregnant that was when it stopped being fun. It was more of an issue because I did not want them, but they wanted my love and affection. But when I realized it was more manipulation that was an issue. It was worse for me as I still had trust issues. I am cutting school now. I played them like they played me.

They would come to my town in someone else car looking for me saying I was their big brother-I was naive. So, I stopped dealing with girls my age and started talking to older women. Now I am going to the mall. I realize the women in the mall had cars- they thought I was 18 or 19. I started dealing with a woman that lived on my grandma's block- the woman's husband was a Marine. She wanted to play so I gave her what she asked for. When he came home, she acted like she did not know me. A woman in a white Benz came to my grandma's house and I asked her what did she want? You acted like you did not know me. She said he just came back, and he is only here for 3 days and then he is going back.

That was the last time we talked. We got together and I performed until she told me to stop. She moved out the next week. That was the last time I messed with a female on my block. Michelle was 5'2, with brown skin and hazel eyes. She had golden brown hair, a small waist, a thick butt, and nice thighs. She had no kids. I told her I was hood. She said I do not mess with hood men I need an entrepreneur. She had a Maserati. She lived in the Hamptons. I almost got arrested as she said I broke into her house. I had to hide in the woods. After this, I did not come home for 2 days. When she came and got me, we spent the night in a hotel. Jennifer had blue eyes and blond hair. She weighed 115 lbs., and she thought I was 35. I stole a car so I could see her every day. She paid for my gas and gave me $400 in cash. If you want to do this, go to the Marriott hotel.

Age 13

This is when the whoring started for me. I met Jennifer at the hotel bar. I had a double shot of Hennessy, and she did too and that started the conversation. It was a lustful business relationship with her, and she treated me well. When she found out my real age, I was 18. From the age of 13, women kept thinking I was older and that lasted until I was 16.

Age 14

I found my Angelika. I never knew how to tell her I was really a bad boy, so she got to see the innocence and the good side of me. In her eyes I was a good guy but, in the streets, I was a demon. I took the demon and enhanced it even more- she did not know I had a reputation. Everything I was doing I kept away from her. I had a gun and crack in my pocket, and I went to church to try to redeem myself-I Jason black Timberlands and a black hoodie in church and I was turned away. When I got turned away, I felt like the streets were my best friend- I did not put my faith in the church but rather in God. I had one foot in God and one foot in the streets. I found a new church that told me to come as you are and that led me to join the choir. I thought I would be happy, but I was just playing myself. I was trying to cover up my demons by going to church and that was the wrong thing to do because I was sheltering the multiple personalities that I had. I was going to church, but I felt guilty, so I cut myself. I was acting like I was too good to be in the streets, but the streets were my home. I was living in falsehood, so I started gang banging.

By Gangbanging with the bloods and crips, I was betraying myself because these were people that I knew and grew up with. This made me trip on myself, so I started self-mutilating. I left the church and went back to the streets. I was accepted so quickly so I thought it would be cool to be who I am. Come to find out the streets don't love nobody. My name got assassinated so I turned it up and started saying neighborhood, so people started asking me what does Neighborhood mean? I told them that it was anywhere I want to go. Any neighborhood I went to was my neighborhood. I shoot first and ask questions later. I asked GOD to forgive me and show me a different life, but my demons were still there, and they played their part- getting drunk, listening to everybody so I banged for my neighborhood and then I realized I did not have to do that anymore so cutting myself was the easiest thing to do- nobody would know. That was when I realized that self-mutilation was an expression of another part of who I am. If I can cut myself what would make you think I would not slit your throat?

This brought me back to who I was. It brought me back to when I could not carry a gun or knife- people would cross the street when they saw me. Fear comes with a lot of responsibility. I was 14 years and beating grown behind men that were preying on women. If I saw a man slap a woman, he got a beat down. That put me into a lot of messed-up situations. I was messing up myself as well as my name. I hit a man and he pulled a gun on me, twice. That made me cold. I said kill me I am ready to die. I do not care about living. I will just be another dead Black man. He asked me how old I was, and I told him I was 14. I told him, "You are not the first person to pull a gun on me!" He asked me if I wanted a job and little did, I know, that this was going to put me back in the game. I had $36000 in counterfeit money every day and I am only 14! I am going to stay with this gig for about a year. I threw a hose party for my 15th birthday. I brought a bottle of Cristal and Alize. I made a drink called Thug Passion where I mixed one-half of Cristal and ¾ of Alize. Everyone except me went to jail at the end of the night. I went to school with a bottle that I forgot I had. I had a hangover and threw up. I got sent to the nurse's office but instead, I went home.

Later on, that day the twins Nivea and Olay came and asked me if I was ok. I handed them a pack of cigarettes and then I left. When I got back to my grandma's house and the phone rang and I accepted the call- I said John came home because he was sick. I had Ray and Nephew before I went to school and Hennessy at midday and another shot of Tay and Nephew before I went to sleep. I did sports for a while in school, but they had me as a benchwarmer, so I quit sports and went back to selling drugs. Angelika still thought I was a good guy. She came to my school one day and a guy was trying to talk to her. I pulled him to the side and told him not to try to talk to her otherwise he will not be running track anymore. As I began talking to Kenifa, Jennifer pulled up to the school in a Benz. It wasn't drug money she was talking about; it was sex money. I asked her to meet me at the Dublin and she showed up at around 10:30 that night.

She told me to stop hi I go around and get back to work at the Marriott. I told her I had a connection that I had to meet up with. She kept asking me what connection but since she was not my woman, I didn't tell her. She told me she had a woman she wanted to introduce me to. Her name is Paprika. Paprika had a girlfriend named Oregano and Jennifer had Paprika as her girlfriend. Oregano smoked hella weed and sniffed more coke than Tony Montana. She made me the most money because she would do anything for me. Oregano got a hold of some bad stuff, and we were at the Coliseum, and she said she wanted some more drugs on consignment. I did not want her to give me sex for the drugs. I later saw her with a needle in her arm, and she was speed balling.

Two weeks later Oregano overdosed. I did not go to the funeral because I felt that her death was my fault. Ever since then I decided to only sell crack cocaine. That was when I realized how to get real money. Now I learned how to cook the drugs because I got tired of paying someone else to do it. I went to one of my kinfolks and asked them if they did drugs and if they knew how to cook crack he smacked me in the face, and then I pulled out my gun, a snub-nosed 38 Smith & Wesson. He said put that shit away. I said, "Are you going to fight bitch?" He said," So nephew you grew the fuck up?". I said, hell yeah, I am not with the kiddie shit. And just for fair warning if you pull out a gun you shoot- use it boy, So I put the gun down and we started tussling! He beat me up!! My Unc was 6'3 and 375 lbs. I am close to 120 lbs. and 5'6. I have him a little run for his money. I caught him in the mouth and made him bleed then his body slammed me. Unc then choked me out. I tapped out and said Ok do now let's get down to business Unc. So Unc asked if he could sample what I had. So, I gave him some of the product and it was yellow.

So Unc said it was fish scale. So, he asked me what I wanted to use to cut it with. He wanted me to choose between alcohol and baking soda. So, I said let us do it half and half said one will be bells and the other one will be ringing your bells. I asked Unc what the difference was. Unc showed me how to cook it, how much to put in, lb99 the percentage of cocaine to water to baking soda. Unc asked if I knew how to deal with alcohol- you put cocaine with alcohol and swirl it around and you get a new product- alcohol burns faster so customers come back quicker.

Oh, thanks Unc! Unc said I got to get my new clientele up-give me a cut of what you got- I am not cooking for free! How much do you want of the cut Unc? Do you want a quarter? I thought he really wanted a quarter, so I gave him $340 worth. He did not need that- he smoked it all up! He brought me one client who I said could talk to everyone else- so that one client brought me $60000 in 4 weeks- I took pennies, nickels, dimes, quarters, and dollars, 24 hours a day when my phone was not on, they called my house. I did not have a car- I rode my bike to deliver. After 12 at night, you had to make a buy of at least $120. I was so happy because everyone called me at 12 midnight- if it was 3 am you had to buy $250 worth. Give it all to me!! Did not matter what the amount was I took ALL COINS!

I did not sleep and was still going to school, so I slept in school. The only way I passed my classes was that I had females helping me. I was retarded and I did not care- I had money! I did not understand education was the key. Now I knew I had to get a job! I got a Union job and was still selling drugs. I am working at the bar and still going to school and trying to maintain a real life as a kid. how the fuck am I supposed to do that? I know that I am bad so how am I not supposed to make money? This is what my grandma and grandfather and great-grandpa taught me My great-grandpa taught me how to hustle. whether it was scrap iron or whatever. I have to say I did not understand what hustle meant as I was still a kid. He showed me laundering moving anything so as a child before school. that was how I learned. one was from the South and one from Jamaica.

Now I found out about rifles. My grandma did not like guns, so I hid my rifle in the closet. She found my rifle in the closet and took it and threw it in the garbage. So, I got another one and hid it in my drawer. Grandma went into my room and went into the drawer and found my gun. I was on my

bike, and she asked me who owned the gun. I

screamed that I needed it for my protection.

grandma said protection from what. she went to the

dumpster and threw my gun in it.

Age 16

I am now 16 years old, and I got sent to jail for extortion. I kept taking everybody's money. When I got to jail there was a strip search. I was a child, and they made me take off all my clothes and spread my legs and made me squat. Nassau County does not care how they do you! They processed and fingerprinted me and put me in a holding cell. I am in the elk by myself, which is cool but to my surprise, they got me on the news! I was on the Channel 12 News for robbery and extortion.

They put me in the system and stuff that I thought had disappeared showed up. Bail was set at $500000. The DA says I am a menace to society.

I said fuck y'all niggers and crackers. because I said that it made me look worse. I was home but I am on felony probation. So, I had to do felony probation for 5 years and then I got in trouble again. I banged out and they called the police on me. On my G a gated status I told them to set it up charges got pressed on me. Now my bail is $500000 again. now it is B and E. I learned how to break into houses. For a window, you pop out the cylinder and when you get inside the house you lock it back. After I get in the house, and everybody is asleep. how would you know if I was there? I watch everyone's movements while they are asleep.

She woke up first and she did not know I was there. she went and took a shower and went to work. When he woke up, she had already left. so, he got tied up and tortured. Cutting out parts of your body means a lot. One of his ears got taken off and I stuffed something up his nose. his nose got cut off and his thumb got burned. He gave me the information I wanted. I found out the connection that tried to kill me! I had sex with his sister, and she had a baby. Shit happens in life!

Age 17

I am 17 now and in Kentucky. these MF do not know who a gangster is. You are not wearing a rod. Why? I wear grey, blue, black, and burgundy. Do you think it is all about red? Are you banging? What am I about? I am about $$$. So, we are about the same thing. OK so here is your gun. I came back to NY and shot 3 people. I am still on 5 years' probation.

I saw my probation officer every week. I kept leaving NY to be with women out of state. I was happy but also sad. I did not love myself, but I loved what I was doing. It took me some time to understand I could do what I want. I realized I needed to talk to GOD. Talking to GOD led me to stop gangbanging. I gave away the guns. In reality, nobody gave a fuck what I did. I went back to extortion. And I asked GOD to watch out for me as I know what I was doing was wrong. I went back to selling crack and I was working in a white neighborhood. I learned they were using heroin so now I am selling crack, cocaine, and heroin. speedball was killing off clients. I got mad because I could not get money, so I started robbing drug dealers. Now it is my 18th birthday. It was a good day! I got to be a kid again! Got to be a kid for 72 whole minutes! You got to go back on the block. why are you not answering my page? I hit hour 2 way and your beeper and your pager. are you trying to rob me? They put me in the basement for 18 hours and were punching and kicking me in my face when it was all over, they said we thought you stole from us. I took my black Timberland boots out of the box and said karma is a bitch. They wanted to kill me! To be continued…

Made in the USA
Middletown, DE
27 May 2023

30839862R00031